This book belongs to

....

Quarto is the authority on a wide range of topics.

Quarto educates, entertains and enriches the lives of our readers—enthusiasts and lovers of hands-on living.

www.quartoknows.com

First published in 2018 by QED Publishing, an imprint of The Quarto Group.
The Old Brewery, 6 Blundell Street, London N7 9BH, United Kingdom.
T (0)20 7700 6700 F (0)20 7700 8066
www.QuartoKnows.com

A catalogue record for this book is available from the British Library.

ISBN 978-1-78493-927-4

Based on the original story by Jessica Barrah and Chris Saunders
Author of adapted text: Katie Woolley
Series Editor: Joyce Bentley
Series Designer: Sarah Peden

Manufactured in Dongguan, China TL102017

9 8 7 6 5 4 3 2 1

MIX
Paper from responsible sources
FSC® C104723

**Reading
Gems**

The Helpful
DRAGON

The villagers of Puddle Village had a problem. It was a large, red fiery problem.

"There's a dragon on the track," shouted the station master.

All the villagers tried to wake it up,
but nothing they did worked.

The dragon just snored and snored.

The villagers gathered on the village green for a meeting.

"There will be a reward for anyone who can move that dragon," said the mayor.

One little girl knew just what to do.

Lucy rode to the train station as fast as she could.

"I want that reward so I can buy a new bike," she said. "I'll move the dragon."

The red, fiery dragon was very, very big! Lucy decided it must be hungry.

"Would you like some food, Mr Dragon?" she asked. Lucy rustled a packet of salt and vinegar crisps.

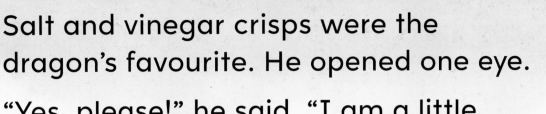

Salt and vinegar crisps were the dragon's favourite. He opened one eye.

"Yes, please!" he said. "I am a little bit hungry."

9

The dragon ate all the crisps in one big gulp! Snap! Snap! Snap!

The trouble was, he was a big dragon.

"I'm still hungry," he said. "Can I have some more food, please?"

"Follow me," said Lucy. "I'm sure we can find some more in the village."

The dragon got up off the track, and the pair went to look for food.

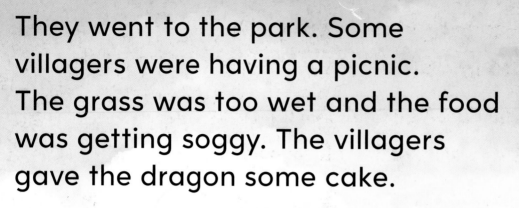

They went to the park. Some villagers were having a picnic. The grass was too wet and the food was getting soggy. The villagers gave the dragon some cake.

Then Lucy had an idea! She whispered in the dragon's ear.

The dragon quickly breathed hot air over the grass. It was soon dry.

He gobbled up some more food but the dragon was still hungry.

13

Lucy and the dragon went to find more food. Nearby, a chef was cooking on a barbeque but he didn't have any fire.

"I know what to do!" said Lucy. She whispered in the dragon's ear again.

Quick as a flash, the dragon breathed fire over the barbeque. It was soon sizzling!

Then, he ate a sausage or two! But, the dragon was still hungry.

On they went. Lucy and the dragon walked into a wedding party. There was lots of food to eat. The dragon licked his lips!

"Hello," said the bride. "I'll give you some food if you warm up my wedding tent."

"Of course!" said the dragon.

He breathed hot air into the tent until it was warm and cosy.

Then, he gobbled up all the buns.

Back at the village green, it was time for the fair.

Lucy's mother had come to the fair to see where Lucy was.

"I'm here!" said Lucy. She and the dragon had come to join the fun at the fair. "The dragon is right here too!"

"Gosh, what a big dragon!" said the mayor.

"Don't worry," said Lucy. "He's a helpful dragon!"

"What a helpful dragon!" said the mayor. "Will you stay in Puddle Village?"

"Yes, please," said the dragon. "I like it here."

The dragon had great fun at the fair. He ate all the food. He even ate Lucy's doughnut!

He lit the village fireworks.
Whizz! Pop! Bang!

"Hooray for the helpful
dragon!" cried the villagers.

Story Words

barbeque

bike

breathed

bride

chef

crisps

dragon

fireworks

food

mayor

reward

sausage

station master

track

wedding

Let's Talk About The Helpful Dragon

Look carefully at the book cover.

Who is in the picture?

What is the dragon doing?

Name some of the food that the dragon is eating.

The dragon is very hungry in the story. He likes to eat all sorts of food.

What food do you like to eat? What is your favourite meal? Is there anything you don't like?

The dragon turns out to be helpful.

Can you remember how he helps the villagers of Puddle Village?

Lucy decides to move the dragon from the train tracks.

Why does she do this? Do you think she got her reward?

Did you like the ending of the story?

What do you think happened next?

Fun and Games

Look back through the story and put these characters in the order they appear.

bride

dragon

Lucy

mayor

station master

chef

Answers: 1 station master; 2 dragon; 3 mayor; 4 Lucy; 5 chef and 6 bride.

Say these words aloud. Does the letter pattern in bold of each pair sound the same or different?

a

dr**a**gon

st**a**tion

b

b**i**k**e**

br**id**e

c

p**air**

f**air**

d

f**i**re

cr**i**sps

Answers: a no; b yes; c yes and d no.

Your Turn

Now that you have read the story,
have a go at telling it in your own words.
Use the pictures below to help you.

GET TO KNOW READING GEMS

Reading Gems is a series of books that has been written for children who are learning to read. The books have been created in consultation with a literacy specialist.

The books fit into four levels, with each level getting more challenging as a child's confidence and reading ability grows. The simple text and fun illustrations provide gradual, structured practice of reading. Most importantly, these books are good stories that are fun to read!

Level 1 is for children who are taking their first steps into reading. Story themes and subjects are familiar to young children, and there is lots of repetition to build reading confidence.

Level 2 is for children who have taken their first reading steps and are becoming readers. Story themes are still familiar but sentences are a bit longer, as children begin to tackle more challenging vocabulary.

Level 3 is for children who are developing as readers. Stories and subjects are varied, and more descriptive words are introduced.

Level 4 is for readers who are rapidly growing in reading confidence and independence. There is less repetition on the page, broader themes are explored and plot lines straddle multiple pages.

The Helpful Dragon follows the dragon's search for food in Puddle Village. It explores themes of friendship and not judging on appearance alone.

Level 4

Back at the village green, it was time for the fair.

Lucy's mother had come to the fair to see where Lucy was too.

"I'm here!" said Lucy. She and the dragon had come to join the fun at the fair. "The dragon is right here!"

Longer sentences ✓

Wide range of vocabulary ✓

Varied and descriptive language ✓

Pictures provide opportunity for further discussion ✓